Pocket Pal

Gross Jokes

D0451985

Gross Jokes

HINKLER
BOOKS

Published by Hinkler Books Pty Ltd
45–55 Fairchild Street
Heatherton Victoria 3202 Australia
www.hinklerbooks.com

© Hinkler Books Pty Ltd 2010

Cover illustration: Rob Kiely
Illustrations: Glen Singleton
Prepress: Splitting Image
Typesetting: MPS Limited

ISBN: 978 1 7418 5789 4

Printed and bound in China

What's green, sticky and
smells like eucalyptus?

Koala vomit.

What is the difference between
broccoli and boogers?

Kids don't like to eat broccoli!

Why did Piglet look in the toilet?

He was looking for Pooh.

What do you call a lion wearing a hat?

A dandy lion.

What's the last thing that goes
through a bug's mind when
he hits a car windscreen?

His bottom.

Why do little brothers chew
with their mouths full?

Flies have to live somewhere.

What do you get if you sit under a cow?

A flat heud.

What is the soft stuff
between sharks' teeth?

Slow swimmers.

Mummy, Mummy, can I lick the bowl?

No! You'll have to flush like everyone else.

What's a sick joke?

Something that comes up in conversation.

Who is the best dancer at a
monster party?

The Boogie Man!

What's the difference between a
maggot and a cockroach?

*Cockroaches crunch more
when you eat them.*

'I just got a bunch of flowers for my wife.'

'Great swap.'

What do you give a sick elephant?

A very big paper bag.

What's brown and sounds like a bell?

Dung.

Why do petrol stations always
lock their toilets?

They are afraid someone might clean them.

What do you do if your
nose goes on strike?

Picket.

What does a boy monster do when a
girl monster rolls her eyes at him?

He rolls them back to her.

How does a monster count to thirteen?

On his fingers.

Mother vampire to son: 'Hurry up and eat your breakfast before it turns into a scab.'

How do you make a tissue dance?

Put some boogie into it.

9

Little Monster: 'I hate my
teacher's guts!'

*Mum Monster: 'Then just eat around
them!'*

Little Monster: 'Should I eat my
fries with my fingers?'

*Mum Monster: 'No, you should
eat them separately!'*

Mum, everyone at school
calls me a werewolf.

Don't worry about it, just comb your face.

What's old, wrinkled and puts
away your underwear?

Your grandma.

How can you tell when a moth farts?

He flies straight for a second.

What do you say when
you meet a toad?

Wart's new?

What has two grey legs and two
brown legs?

An elephant with diarrhoea.

What makes you seasick?

Your little brother's vomit.

How many balls of string would it
take to get to the moon?

One, if it's long enough.

What do you call a crazy spaceman?
An astronut!

What do you call a space magician?
A flying sorcerer!

THE GREATEST MAGIC SHOW IN THE UNIVERSE!

13

What's another name for a snail?

A booger with a crash helmet.

What's yellow and smells of bananas?

Monkey vomit.

What's green and red and goes at 120 km/h?

A frog in a blender.

What has fifty legs and can't walk?

Half a centipede.

'Daddy, can I have another
glass of water, please?'

*'Okay, but that's the twelfth one
you've had tonight.'*

'Yes I know, but my bedroom
is still on fire.'

What's the difference between school
lunches and a pile of slugs?

School lunches are on plates.

Awwr... I've got SLUGS
again! You don't want to
swap do you?

Did you hear about the two fat men
who ran a marathon?

One ran in short bursts,
the other ran in burst shorts.

What colour is a hiccup?
Burple.

A woman woke her husband
in the middle of the night.

*'There's a burglar in the kitchen eating the
cake I made this morning!' she said.*

*'Who should I call?' asked her husband.
'The police or an ambulance?'*

My cousin spent a lot on deodorant,
until he found out people just didn't
like him.

Did you hear about the two bodies
cremated at the same time?

It was a dead heat.

When the fat man was run over by a
steamroller, what was proved?

That he had a lot of guts.

Boy: 'Dad, there's a black cat in
the dining room!'

Dad: 'That's okay, Son, black cats are lucky.'

Son: 'This one is – he ate your dinner!'

The cruise ship passenger was feeling really seasick, when the waiter asked if she'd like some lunch.

'No thanks,' she replied. 'Just throw it over the side and save me the trouble.'

If you were making a large omelette, would you use chicken eggs or elephant eggs?

Chicken eggs! Elephant yolks are so bad.

She's so ugly, when a wasp stings her, it has to shut its eyes!

There's no point in telling some people a joke with a double meaning. They wouldn't understand either of them!

Geosrge is the type of boy that his mother doesn't want him to hang around with.

Three guys, Shut-up, Manners and Poop, drove too fast and Poop fell out of the car. Shut-up went to the police station, where the policeman asked, 'What's your name?'

'Shut-up,' he answered.

'Hey – where are your manners!' the policeman exclaimed.

Shut-up replied, 'Outside on the road, scrapin' up Poop!'

21

My dad once stopped a man from
hurting a donkey.

It was a case of brotherly love.

Three girls walked into a beauty salon.
Two had blonde hair and one had green
hair. The hairdresser asked the blondes,
'Did you dye your hair blonde?'

'Oh, it's natural,' they replied.

The hairdresser asked the other girl,
'Did you dye your hair green?'

*She replied, 'Oh, it's natural. I put my hand
on my nose and rubbed it into my hair.'*

An astronaut and a chimp rocketed into space. The chimp opened its sealed orders and, as it read them, it started pushing buttons and programming the flight computers.

When the astronaut opened his sealed envelope, his orders read:

'Feed the chimp.'

What do you get when you cross a vampire with a dwarf?

A monster that sucks blood out of people's kneecaps.

The mother monster asked her son what he was doing with a saw, and if he'd seen his brother.

'You mean my new half-brother, Mum,' he replied!

What do you give an elephant with diarrhoea?

Plenty of room.

A woman was facing the judge, charged with wounding her husband.

'You're very lucky you're not facing a murder charge – why did you stab him over and over?' asked the judge.

'I didn't know how to turn off the electric carving knife,' she replied.

Roger was in a full bus when an extremely large lady opposite said to him, 'If you were a gentleman, you'd stand up and let someone else sit down.'

'And if you were a lady,' Roger replied, 'you'd stand up and let four people sit down!'

Did you hear the joke about the fart?

It stinks.

Someone stole all the toilet seats from the police station. The officers have nothing to go on.

Teacher: 'How were your holidays, Penny?'

Penny: 'Great. My brother and I spent the whole time on the beach, burying each other in the sand.'

Teacher: 'That sounds like fun.'

Penny: 'Daddy says we can go back next year and find him.'

What baseball position did the boy with no arms or legs play?

First base.

What did the first mate see in the toilet?

The captain's log.

Why do hot dogs have such bad manners?

They spit in the frying pan.

Take that you filthy bad mannered brutes!!

What do Eskimos get from sitting on
the ice too long?

Polaroids.

Three kids were playing in a park
when a genie appeared. The genie
said they could have one wish each,
as long as they made the wish
while coming down the slide.
The first kid slid down shouting,
'I want a big glass of lemonade.'
The second kid slid down shouting,
'I want a chocolate milkshake.'
The third kid slid down shouting,
'Weeeeee.'

What do you call a boy who eats his
mother and his father?

An orphan.

What is black and white,
and red all over?

A nun in a blender.

What is twenty feet long
and smells musty?

Line dancing at the old people's home.

What dance do hippies hate?

A square dance.

What has four legs and an arm?

A happy lion.

What's green and slimy,
and hangs from trees?

Giraffe boogers.

What do you get if you cross an
elephant with a box of laxatives?

Out of the way.

What's green, has two legs, and sits
on the end of your finger?

The boogeyman.

What's Mozart up to now?

Decomposing.

What's invisible and
smells like carrots?

Bunny farts!

What's the difference between an oral thermometer and a rectal thermometer?

The taste.

Why did the boy take his own toilet paper to the birthday party?

Because he was a party pooper.

Why do farts smell?

*So that deaf people can appreciate
them too.*

What do you find up a clean nose?

Fingerprints.

Why don't elephants pick their noses?

*Because they don't know what to do
with 20-kilogram boogers.*

Why do gorillas have big nostrils?
Because they have big fingers.

Why did the toilet paper roll
down the hill?
To get to the bottom.

Where do lepers shop?
At the secondhand store.

Why did the surfer stop surfing?

Because the sea weed.

What is a cannibal's favourite soup?

One with a lot of body.

First Cannibal: 'My girlfriend's a tough old bird.'

Second Cannibal: 'You should have left her in the oven for another half hour.'

First Cannibal: 'Who was that girl I saw you with last night?'

Second Cannibal: 'That was no girl, that was my dinner.'

First Cannibal: 'How do you make an explorer stew?'

Second Cannibal: 'Keep him waiting a few hours.'

Did you hear about the cannibal who gnawed a bone for hours on end?

When he stood up, he fell over.

How can you help a hungry cannibal?

Give him a hand.

Two cannibals were having lunch.

'Your girlfriend makes a great soup,' said one to the other.

'Yes!' agreed the first. 'But I'm going to miss her!'

What did the cannibal say to the explorer?

'Nice to eat you.'

Why did the cannibal have two plates for dinner?

He wanted a balanced diet.

What did the cannibal say when he
saw Dr. Livingstone?

'Dr. Livingstone, I consume.'

What did the cannibal say when he
was full?

'I couldn't eat another mortal.'

What do the guests do at
a cannibal wedding?

Toast the bride and groom.

Mr Cannibal: 'I'm bringing a friend home for dinner.'

Mrs Cannibal: 'But I've already made dinner.'

What do vegetarian cannibals eat?

Swedes.

What does a cannibal say when a bus load of tourists drives past?

'Smorgasbord.'

What's the favourite game at a cannibal's birthday party?

Swallow the leader.

43

What was the cannibal called, who
ate her father's sister?

An aunt-eater!

Where do cannibals work?

At head office.

Did you hear about the cannibal who
carried on the family traditions?

He swallowed in his father's footsteps.

Why did the cannibal kidnap
the tourist?

He wanted takeaway food.

Why did the cannibal live on his own?

He'd had his fill of other people.

Why don't cannibals eat
weather forecasters?

Because they give them wind.

When the cannibal crossed the Pacific on a cruise ship, she told the waiter to take the menu away and bring her the passenger list!

Mummy, I don't want to go to Europe.

Just keep swimming.

Mummy, Mummy, Dad has been run
over by a steamroller.

Just slide him under the door.

Mummy, Mummy, Daddy's on fire.

Quick! Go get the marshmallows!

Mummy, Mummy, what's a vampire?

Eat your soup before it clots.

Mummy, Mummy, why do I keep
going round in circles?

*Be quiet or I'll nail your
other foot to the floor.*

Mummy, Mummy, are you sure
you bake bread this way?

*Just get back in.
I can't close the oven door.*

Mummy, Mummy, can I play
with Rover?

*We've already dug him up
three times this week.*

Mummy, Mummy, my head hurts.

Then don't stand in front of the dartboard.

Mummy, Mummy, I think I have a
split personality.

Then clean up your brother's room too.

Mummy, Mummy, Daddy just put
Rover down.

I'm sure he had a good reason for it.

But he promised I could do it.

Mummy, Mummy, Daddy's
hammering on the roof again.

I'll just drive a little faster.

Mummy, Mummy, I can't
find the dog's food.

Don't worry about it. Eat your stew.

Mummy, Mummy, I feel like a yoyo.

*Sit down . . .
and up . . . and down . . .*

Mummy, Mummy, I have a splinter in my finger!

Scratching your head again?

Mummy, Mummy, I hate my brother's guts.

Just eat what's on your plate.

Mummy, Mummy, what are you
doing with that axe . . .

Mummy, Mummy, when are we
going to have Grandma for dinner?

*We haven't finished eating
your father yet.*

Mummy, Mummy, I just chopped
off my foot.

Then hop out of the kitchen.

I just mopped the floor.

Mummy, Mummy, why are we pushing the car off the cliff?

Shhh! You'll wake your father.

Mummy, Mummy, why can't we give Grandma a proper burial?

Oh just keep flushing.

Mummy, Mummy, why is Dad running in zigzags?

Just keep shooting.

Mummy, Mummy, why can't we buy a garbage disposal?

You're doing a fine job chewing.

Doctor, Doctor, I feel like a tennis racquet.

You must be too highly strung.

Doctor, Doctor, my nose is running.

You'd better catch it quick.

Doctor, Doctor, I'm afraid of the dark.

Then leave the light on.

Doctor, Doctor, I keep stealing things.

Take one of these pills and if that doesn't work, bring me a computer.

Doctor, Doctor, my stomach hurts.
Stop your belly aching.

Doctor, Doctor, I have a hoarse throat.
The resemblance doesn't end there.

Doctor, Doctor, I keep thinking
I'm a yoyo.

How are you feeling?

Oh, up and down.

Doctor, Doctor, how can I stop
my nose from running?

Stick your foot out and trip it.

Doctor, Doctor, people keep
disagreeing with me.

No they don't.

Doctor, Doctor, I'm at death's door.
Don't worry, I'll pull you through.

Doctor, Doctor, I feel like
a pair of socks.
Well I'll be darned.

Doctor, Doctor, I keep thinking
I'm a doorknob.

Well, don't fly off the handle.

Doctor, Doctor, I'm a wrestler
and I feel awful.

Get a grip on yourself.

Doctor, Doctor, I think I'm a video.

I thought I'd seen you before.

Doctor, Doctor, I feel funny today.
What should I do?

Become a comedian?

Doctor, Doctor, I think
I've been bitten by a vampire.

Drink this glass of water.

Will it make me better?

*No, but I'll be able to see
if your neck leaks!*

Doctor, Doctor, will you treat me?

No, you'll have to pay like everybody else.

Doctor, Doctor, I keep thinking I'm a $100 note.

Go shopping, the change will do you good.

Doctor, Doctor, I swallowed a spoon.

Well try to relax and don't stir.

Doctor, Doctor, I swallowed a roll of film.

Don't worry, nothing will develop.

Doctor, Doctor, nobody ever listens to me.

Next!

Doctor, Doctor, I have not stopped laughing since my operation!

That surgeon always has people in stitches.

Doctor, Doctor, I'm so ugly – what can I do about it?

Hire yourself out for Halloween parties.

Doctor, Doctor, I'm as sick as a dog.

Well, I can't help you because I'm not a vet.

Doctor, Doctor, my eyesight is getting worse.

You're absolutely right, this is a post office.

Doctor, Doctor, the first thirty minutes I'm up every morning I feel dizzy, what should I do?

Get up half an hour later.

Doctor, Doctor, what does this X-ray of my head show?

Unfortunately, nothing.

Doctor, Doctor, this ointment you gave me makes my arm smart!

Try putting some on your head.

Doctor, Doctor, something is preying on my mind!

Don't worry, it will probably starve to death.

Doctor, Doctor, I feel like a bell.

Well, take these and if they don't work, give me a ring.

Doctor, Doctor, I have a ringing
in my ears!

Well, answer it.

Doctor, Doctor, every time I stand
up I see visions of Mickey Mouse and
Pluto and every time I sit down I see
Donald Duck!

*How long have you been having these
Disney spells?*

Doctor, Doctor, it hurts when I do this!

Well, don't do that.

Doctor, Doctor, I snore so loud,
I wake myself up!

Try sleeping in another room.

Doctor, Doctor, my leg hurts,
what can I do?

Limp.

Doctor, Doctor, I have yellow teeth,
what should I do?

Wear a brown tie.

Doctor, Doctor, I feel like a dog.

Then go see a vet!

Doctor, Doctor, I have a pain in my eye every time I drink hot chocolate.

Take the spoon out of your mug before you drink.

Doctor, Doctor, can you help me out?

Certainly – which way did you come in?

Doctor, Doctor, I dreamed that
I ate a large marshmallow!

Did you wake up without a pillow?

Doctor, Doctor, my brother thinks
he's a chicken.

How long has this been going on?

About six months.

Why didn't you bring him here earlier?

We needed the eggs.

Doctor, Doctor, I feel like a dog.

Sit!

Doctor, Doctor, I keep thinking
I'm a dog.

How long has this been going on?

Ever since I was a pup.

Doctor, Doctor, did you hear about the boy who swallowed a coin?

No? Well, there's no change yet!

Doctor, Doctor, my son swallowed a pen, what should I do?

Use a pencil instead!

Doctor, Doctor, my wooden leg is giving me a lot of pain.

Why's that?

My wife keeps hitting me over the head with it!

Doctor, Doctor, my hair is falling out, can you give me something to keep it in?

Yes, a paper bag.

Doctor, Doctor, my belly is so big that I'm embarrassed by it. What can I do?

Have you tried to diet?

Yes, but the different colours do not seem to make a difference.

Doctor, Doctor, I have a terrible cough!

Then you should practise.

Doctor, Doctor, I keep thinking I'm a dog.

Well, get up on the couch and I'll examine you.

I can't, I'm not allowed on the furniture.

Doctor, Doctor, I feel like a piano.

Wait a minute while I take some notes.

Doctor, Doctor, will my measles
be better by next Monday?

I don't want to make any rash promises.

Doctor, Doctor, I keep thinking
I'm a fruitcake.

What's got into you?

Flour, raisins and cherries.

Doctor, Doctor, my wife thinks I'm
crazy because I like hamburgers.

That's ridiculous. I like hamburgers too.

Good, you should come by and see
my collection some time. I have
hundreds of them.

Doctor, Doctor, I keep hearing a ringing in my ears.

Where did you expect to hear it?

Doctor, Doctor, what's good for biting fingernails?

Very sharp teeth.

Doctor, Doctor, I have a carrot growing out of my ear.

Amazing! How did that happen?

I don't know – I planted cabbages in there!

Doctor, Doctor, can you give me anything for excessive wind?

Sure, here's a kite.

Doctor, Doctor, can I have a bottle of aspirin and a pot of glue?

Why?

Because I have a splitting headache!

Doctor, Doctor, should I surf the Internet on an empty stomach?

No, you should do it on a computer.

Doctor, Doctor, my girlfriend
thinks she's a duck.

*You'd better bring her
in to see me right away.*

I can't – she's already
flown south for the winter.

Doctor, Doctor, everyone hates me.

*Don't be stupid, not everyone
has met you yet.*

Doctor, Doctor, I feel like a toad.

Don't worry! We have hoperations for that these days.

Doctor, Doctor, my little brother thinks he's a computer.

Well, bring him in so I can cure him.

I can't, I need to use him to finish my homework!

Doctor, Doctor, my wife thinks she's a chicken.

Do you want me to cure her?

No, I just wondered if you wanted some eggs.

Doctor, Doctor, I have a sore throat.

Open your mouth and stick your tongue out facing the window.

What's that have to do with my sore throat?

Nothing. I just don't like my neighbours.

Doctor, Doctor, I was playing a kazoo and I swallowed it.

Lucky you weren't playing the piano.

Doctor, Doctor, I think I'm a bridge.

What's come over you?

Oh, two cars, a large truck and a bus.

Doctor, Doctor, when I press with my
finger here . . . it hurts, and here . . .
it hurts, and here . . .
and here! What do you
think is wrong with me?

Your finger's broken.

Doctor, Doctor, I think
I'm a mouse trap!

Well, snap out of it.

Doctor, Doctor, I have flowers
growing out
of the top of my head.

Don't worry, it's just a beauty spot.

Doctor, Doctor, have you
taken my temperature?

No. Is it missing?

Doctor, Doctor, I get so nervous when I drive I keep bumping into things!

Don't worry, I'll prescribe a crash course!

Doctor, Doctor, I feel like a pack of cards.

I'll deal with you later.

Doctor, Doctor, I've just
swallowed a pen.

Well, sit down and fill out this form!

Doctor, Doctor, my sister thinks
she's a squirrel.

Sounds like a nut case to me.

Doctor, Doctor, I feel like an apple.

We must get to the core of this!

Doctor, Doctor, I feel like a sheep.

That's baaaaaaaaaaad!

Doctor, Doctor, I'm becoming invisible.

Yes, I can see you're not all there!

Doctor, Doctor, I'm covered in spots.

Let's not do anything rash!

Doctor, Doctor, everyone keeps throwing me in the garbage.

Don't talk rubbish!

Doctor, Doctor, I'm turning into a wastebasket.

Don't give me a bunch of garbage.

Doctor, Doctor, I'm boiling up!

Just simmer down!

Doctor, Doctor, I feel like a needle.

I see your point!

Doctor, Doctor, how can
I cure my sleepwalking?

Sprinkle tacks on your bedroom floor!

Doctor, Doctor, I feel like a racehorse.

Take one of these every four laps!

Doctor, Doctor. . .

You need new glasses.

But I haven't told you what's wrong with me yet.

I could tell as soon as you walked in through the window.

Doctor, Doctor, I'm a burglar!

Have you taken anything for it?

Doctor, Doctor, I need some
acetylsalicylic acid.

You mean aspirin?

That's it. I can never
remember that word.

Doctor, Doctor, I feel like an apple.

Well don't worry, I won't bite.

An apple
a day didn't
keep me
away from
the doctor's!

Doctor, Doctor, my tongue tingles when I touch it to an unsalted peanut wrapped in aluminium foil. What's wrong with me?

You have far too much free time.

Doctor, Doctor, I tend to flush a lot.

Don't worry, it's just a chain reaction.

Doctor, Doctor, will this ointment clear up my spots?

I never make rash promises!

Doctor, Doctor, I think I'm a moth.

So why did you come by?

Well, I saw your light on.

Doctor, Doctor, I keep thinking
I'm a spider.

What a web of lies!

Doctor, Doctor, I think I'm a snail.

*Don't worry, we'll have
you out of your shell soon.*

Doctor, Doctor, I think I'm an adder.

*Great, can you help me with
my accounts please?*

Doctor, Doctor, I keep painting
myself gold.

Don't worry, it's just a gilt complex.

Doctor, Doctor, my baby looks
just like his father.

Don't worry — as long as he's healthy.

Doctor, Doctor, I'm scared. This is my
first operation.

*I know how you feel, it's the first time
I've done one!*

Doctor, Doctor, I keep thinking there's two of me.

One at a time please!

Doctor, Doctor, some days I feel like a teepee and other days I feel like a wigwam.

You're too tents!

Doctor, Doctor, my little boy just swallowed a roll of film.

Hmmm. Let's hope nothing develops!

Doctor, Doctor, I keep thinking
I'm a computer.

*My goodness, you'd better come to my
office right away!*

I can't, my power cable won't reach
that far!

Doctor, Doctor, I don't think I'm a
computer any more. Now I
think I'm a desk.

You're just letting things get on top of you.

Doctor, Doctor, my sister keeps
thinking she's invisible.

Which sister?

Doctor, Doctor, how much to have
this splinter taken out?

Seventy dollars.

Seventy dollars for just a
couple of minutes' work?

I can pull it out very slowly if you like.

Doctor, Doctor, I dream there are
zombies under my bed.
What can I do?

Saw the legs off your bed.

Doctor, Doctor, I think I'm a yoyo.

You're stringing me along!

Doctor, Doctor, I keep thinking
I'm a vampire.

Necks, please!

Doctor, Doctor, I think I'm an electric eel.

That's shocking!

Doctor, Doctor, I think I'm a woodworm.

How boring for you!

Doctor, Doctor, I swallowed a bone.

Are you choking?

No, I really did!

Doctor, Doctor, I need something
for my temper.

Just wait 'til you get the bill.

Doctor, Doctor, I keep thinking
I'm a mosquito.

What a sucker!

Doctor, Doctor, I've broken
my arm in two places.

Well, don't go back there again.

Doctor, Doctor, I think I'm a frog.

What's wrong with that?

I think I'm going to croak!

Doctor, Doctor, I think
I'm a caterpillar.

Don't worry, you'll change soon.

Doctor, Doctor, I think I'm a snake,
about to shed my skin.

Why don't you go behind the screen and
slip into something more comfortable!

Doctor, Doctor, these pills you
gave me for body odour. . .

What's wrong with them?

They keep slipping out from
under my arms!

Doctor, Doctor, my husband
smells like a fish.

Poor sole!

Doctor, Doctor, my sister thinks she's
a lift.

Well, tell her to come in.

I can't, she doesn't stop on this floor!

Doctor, Doctor, I think I'm a moth.
Get out of the way, you're in my light!

Doctor, Doctor, how long have I got?
Ten.
Ten what? Ten months? Ten weeks?
10, 9, 8, 7...

Doctor, Doctor, how was my check-up?

Perfect. You'll live to be 80.

But I am 80.

In that case, it's been nice knowing you.

Doctor, Doctor, do you have something for a migraine?

Take this hammer and hit yourself on the foot. You'll forget about your headache.

Doctor, Doctor, I ate some oysters and now I'm feeling sick.

Were they fresh?

How can you tell?

You open the shell and look.

You're not supposed to eat the shell?

Doctor, Doctor, I came as quick as I could. What's the problem?

Your lab results are back and you only have 24 hours to live.

That's terrible.

There's worse news. I've been trying to call you since yesterday.

Doctor, Doctor, I get very nervous and scared during driving tests.

Don't worry, you'll pass eventually.

But I'm the examiner!

Doctor, Doctor, I can't feel my legs.

That's because we had to amputate your arms.

Doctor, Doctor, I feel like a bird.

I'll tweet you in a minute.

Doctor, Doctor, I feel like a strawberry.

I can see you're in a bit of a jam.

Doctor, Doctor, I think I'm a rubber band.

Why don't you stretch yourself out on the couch there, and tell me all about it?

Doctor, Doctor, I keep seeing double.

Please hop up on the table.

Which one?

Doctor, Doctor, I keep seeing green aliens with two heads and four legs.

Have you seen a psychiatrist?

No, just green aliens with two heads and four legs.

Doctor, Doctor, I keep thinking I'm a bee.

Buzz off, I'm busy.

Doctor, Doctor, my wife keeps beating me.

Oh dear. How often?

Every time we play Scrabble.

Doctor, Doctor, I think I'm a nit.

Will you get out of my hair?

Some patients just get in your hair...

Doctor, Doctor, I've lost my memory!
When did this happen?
When did what happen?

Doctor, Doctor, I think I'm a clock.
You're winding me up.

Doctor, Doctor, I think I'm invisible.
Come back later. I can't see you now.

Doctor, Doctor, I think
I'm losing my mind.

Don't worry, you won't miss it.

Doctor, Doctor, I think
I'm turning into a woman.

Well, you are 16 now Amanda.

Doctor, Doctor, I think I'm
suffering from déjà vu.

Haven't I seen you before?

Doctor, Doctor, I feel like
a pair of curtains.

Well, pull yourself together.

Doctor, Doctor, I think I'm a python.

*You can't get around me
like that, you know!*

Doctor, Doctor, my pig has a rash.
What should I do?

Try this oinkment.

Doctor, Doctor, I have jelly in my ear.

You're just a trifle deaf.

Doctor, Doctor, my baby swallowed
some explosives.

*Well, keep calm. We don't
want him to go off.*

Doctor, Doctor, I think I'm a computer.

How long have you felt like this?

Ever since I was switched on!

Doctor, Doctor, why are you so short-tempered?

I don't have enough patients.

Doctor, Doctor, my son swallowed my razor blade.

Well, just use an electric razor.

Doctor, Doctor, my wife's contractions are only five minutes apart.

Is this her first child?

No, this is her husband.

Doctor, Doctor, should I file my nails?

*No, throw them away like
everyone else does.*

Doctor, Doctor, since the operation
on my leg, I lean one way.

I think you're all right.

Doctor, Doctor, sometimes
I feel like a goat.

How long has this been going on?

Ever since I was a kid.

Doctor, Doctor, I can't get to sleep.

*Sit on the edge of the bed and
you'll drop off.*

CLUNK

Doctor, Doctor, sometimes I feel like
an onion, and sometimes I feel like a
cucumber.

Boy, you're in a pickle.

Doctor, Doctor, sometimes
I think I'm a biscuit.

Just a little crackers, huh?

Doctor, Doctor, sometimes I think
there are two of me.

*Good, you can pay both bills on
your way out.*

Doctor, Doctor, tell me straight.
Is it bad?

*Just don't start watching any
new TV series.*

Doctor, Doctor, will I be able to play the guitar when my hand heals?

Of course.

Great. Because I couldn't play it before.

124

Doctor, Doctor, what's wrong
with me?

Well, you have a carrot up your nose,
a bean in one ear, and a French fry in the
other. I'd say you're not eating right.

'Can I go swimming now, Mum?'
asked the child.

'No – there are sharks out there,'
said his mother.

'Dad's swimming!'

'Yes, he's got a million dollars' life insurance.'

Doctor, Doctor, you've taken out my tonsils, my appendix, my gall bladder and one of my kidneys, but I still feel sick.

That's enough out of you.

Doctor, Doctor, I have a split personality.

Well, you'd better both sit down, then.

Waiter, what kind of soup is this?

Bean soup.

I don't care what it's been. What is it now?

Waiter, there's a fly in my soup!

Don't worry sir, the spider in your salad will get it!

Waiter, I'm in a hurry. Will my pizza be long?

No, it will be round.

Waiter, this soup tastes funny.
Why aren't you laughing then?

Waiter, this egg is bad.
Well don't blame me, I only laid the table.

Waiter, there's a bug
in my soup.
*Be quiet, sir, or everyone
will want one.*

Waiter, how long will my
hot dogs be?

Oh, about 20 centimetres.

Waiter, you have your thumb
on my steak!

Well I didn't want to drop it again.

Waiter, there's a fly in my soup.

Yes sir, the hot water killed it.

Waiter, how did this fly get in
my soup?

It flew.

Waiter, I can't eat this meal.
Please get the manager.

It's no use. He won't eat it either.

Waiter, do you have frog legs?

Yes sir.

Then hop to the kitchen, and
fetch me a steak.

Waiter, I'd like my steak burned,
soggy chips, and a grimy, bitter salad.

*I'm afraid the chef won't cook that
for you, sir.*

Why not? He did yesterday.

Waiter, I'll have the burger please.

With pleasure.

No, with fries.

Waiter, I'll have the lamb chops.
And make them lean.

Certainly sir. To the right or the left?

Waiter, what is this fly doing
in my soup?

It looks like the backstroke.

That's his 4th lap and he just keeps going!!

Waiter, I'll have the soup
and fish please.

*I would recommend you eat the fish first.
It's been sitting around for a few days
and is beginning to smell.*

Waiter, is there any soup on the menu?

No madam, I've wiped it all off.

Waiter, is this beef or lamb?

Can't you taste the difference?

No.

Then it doesn't matter.

Waiter, please remove this fly.

But he hasn't finished yet.

Waiter, there's a cockroach in my soup.

Sorry sir, we're all out of flies.

Waiter, there's a dead fly swimming in my soup.

That can't be, sir. Dead flies can't swim.

Waiter, do you serve crabs
at this restaurant?

Yes sir, we serve anyone.

Waiter, there's a fly in my soup.

No sir, that's a cockroach.
The fly is on your roll.

Waiter, there's a fly in my soup.

That's because the chef used to be a tailor.

Waiter, there's a fly in my soup.

Would you prefer him with your main
course?

Waiter, there's a fly on my steak.

*That's because it's attracted to
rotting meat.*

Waiter, there's a spider in my soup.

It must have eaten the fly.

Waiter, this apple pie is smashed.

*Well, you told me to step on it
because you were in a hurry.*

Waiter, this crab only has one claw.

It must have been in a fight.

Then bring me the winner.

Waiter, this coffee tastes like mud.

I can't understand why. It was ground just a minute ago.

Waiter, we'll have two coffees please. And I want a clean cup.

Yes, sir. Here are your two coffees. Now which one of you wanted the clean cup?

Waiter, do you have frog legs?

No, I've always walked like this.

Waiter, there is a small insect in my soup!

Sorry sir, I'll get you a bigger one!

What do you call

... a man who likes to work out?
Jim!

... a boy with really short hair?
Sean!

... a woman with a cat on her head?
Kitty!

. . . **a** woman with one leg?

Eileen!

. . . **a** boy hanging on the wall?

Art!

. . . **a** man with a map on his head?

Miles!

. . . **a** man with a spade?

Doug!

. . . **a** man without a spade?

Douglas!

142

. . . **a** man who owes money?
Bill!

. . . **a** man in a pile of leaves?
Russell!

. . . **a** woman in the distance?
Dot!

. . . **S**omeone who greets you at
your door every morning?

Matt!

. . . **a** man pouring water into
a jug?

Phil!

. . . **a** man with a plank on
his head?

Edward!

. . . **a** girl with a frog on her head?

Lily!

. . . **a** man with a seagull on
his head?

Cliff!

. . . **a** man with a large black and
blue mark on his leg?

Bruce!

. . . **a** man with a licence plate on his head?

Reg!

. . . **a** man with a stamp on his head?

Frank!

. . . **a** woman with a toilet
on her head?

Lu!

. . . **a** woman with two toilets
on her head?

Lulu!

. . . **a** woman with a breeze on
her head?

Gail!

. . . **a** woman with a tortoise
on her head?

Shelley!

. . . **a** woman with a twig
on her head?

Hazel!

. . . **a** man with a kilt on his head?

Scott!

. . . **a** man with a legal document
on his head?

Will!

. . . **a** woman with a Christmas
tree on her head?

Carol!

. . . **a** man with a Christmas
tree on his head?

Noel!

. . . **a** man with a truck on his head?

Deceased!

. . . **a** man with some cat scratches?

Claude!

. . . **a** girl with one foot on each side of a river?

Bridget!

. . . **a** woman who climbs up walls?

Ivy!

. . . **a** man with rabbits in his pants?

Warren!

. . . **a** man who is always around
when you need him?

Andy!

. . . **a** man floating in the sea?

Bob!

. . . **a** superhero that got run over by a steamroller?

Flatman!

. . . **a** Russian gardener?

Ivanhoe!

'Can't Sleep at Night'
by Constance Snoarer

'Chinese Lanterns'
by Eric Trician

'Confessions of a Thief'
by I Dunnit

'Falling from a Height'
by Eileen Toofar

'Maths for Beginners'
by Algy Brar

'Fighting off Burglars'
by Al Sayshun

'Housing Problem'
by Rufus Quick

'My Holiday with the Penguins'
by Anne Tarctic

'Pants Down'
by Lucy Lastic

'The Greediest Monster'
by Buster Gutt

'Foaming at the Mouth'
by Dee Monic

'In the Cannibal's Cauldron'
by Mandy Ceased

'My Crystal Ball'
by CA Lot

'A Time for Witch Hunting'
by Mae B Tomorrow

'The Long Sleep'
by Anna Sthetic

'The Rag and Bone Trade'
by Orson Cart

'Town Planning'
by Sir Veyor

'How to Keep Out a Vampire'
by Dora Steele

'My Life as a Jockey'
by Rhoda Horse

160

What will Bob the Builder be
called when he retires?

Bob.

Person 1: 'Why are you wearing garlic
around your neck?'

Person 2: 'It keeps away vampires.'

Person 1: 'But there aren't any vampires.'

Person 2: 'See, it works.'

A ghost walks into a bar.

*Bartender: 'Sorry, we don't
serve spirits here.'*

Did you hear about the ghosts' race?

It was a dead heat.

Did you hear about the vampire comedian?

He specialised in biting satire.

Did you hear about the vampire who got taken away in a straightjacket?

He went batty.

Did you hear about the
weather wizard?

He's forecasting sunny spells.

Do zombies like the dark?

Of corpse they do.

How can you tell if a corpse is angry?

It flips its lid.

What do you get if you cross a
dinosaur with a vampire?

A blood shortage.

How can you tell what a ghost
is getting for its birthday?

By feeling its presence.

How do you greet a three-headed
monster?

'Hello, hello, hello.'

How do you make a witch itch?

Take away the W.

How does a yeti feel when it
gets a cold?

Abominable.

How does Dracula eat his food?

In bite-sized pieces.

Police Officer 1: 'Where's the skeleton?'

Police Officer 2: 'I had to let him go.'

Police Officer 1: 'But he's our main suspect.'

Police Officer 2: 'I know. But I couldn't pin anything on him.'

What did Frankenstein do when he saw the monster catcher approaching?

He bolted.

What is Dracula's favourite fruit?

Necktarines!

What did the alien say to her son
when he returned home?

'Where on Earth have you been?'

What did the alien say to the plant?

'Take me to your weeder.'

What is the first thing a monster does
when you give him an axe?

Make out a chopping list.

What did the sea monster say when it
saw the brand-new cruise ship sail past?

'Yum. Launch time.'

What do goblin children do after school?

Their gnomework.

What do little zombies play?
Corpse and robbers.

What do monsters have mid-morning?
A coffin break.

Why don't people kiss vampires?
Because they have bat breath.

What vehicles race at the Witches'
Formula One Grand Prix?

Vroomsticks.

What do sea monsters eat?

Fish and ships.

What do vampires have for a snack?

Blood oranges.

What do you call a three-metre-long, two-headed monster?

Anything it wants.

What do you call a detective skeleton?

Sherlock Bones.

What do you call a ghost's
mum and dad?

Transparents.

What do you call a hairy beast in a river?

A weir-wolf.

What do you call a witch
without a broomstick?

A witch-hiker.

What do you do if you're surrounded
by a witch, a werewolf, a vampire
and two ghosts?

Hope you're at a costume party.

What does a monster say when
introduced?

'Pleased to eat you.'

mmm,
breakfast!

175

Why should you never touch
a monster's tail?

It's the end of the monster and the end of you.

What do you call a skeleton who
sits around doing nothing?

Lazy bones.

What do zombies use to make cakes?

Self-raising flour.

What does a monster call his parents?

Dead and mummy.

What does a vampire never
order at a restaurant?

Stake.

Why didn't the undertaker
bury the skeleton?

He didn't have the guts.

How many monsters would it take to fill up your classroom?

I don't know. I wouldn't hang around to find out.

What happened to the naughty school witch?

She was ex-spelled.

What did the witch say to
the vampire?

'Get a life!'

What happened when the
gravediggers went on strike?

Their job was done by a skeleton crew.

What is a vampire's favourite sport?
Batminton.

What is a witch's favourite movie?
'Broom with a View.'

What is Dr. Jekyll's favourite game?
Hyde and seek.

What is Dracula's car called?

A blood mobile.

What is the favourite fair
ride for little ghosts?

The rollerghoster.

What is the first part of a newspaper
that a ghost turns to?

The horror-scope.

What did the ghost buy for his wife?

A see-through nightie.

What kind of plate does a
skeleton eat off?

Bone china.

What kind of cheese do
monsters eat?

Monsterella!

What song did the band play at the
Demons and Ghouls ball?

'Demons are a Ghoul's Best Friend.'

What trees do ghosts like best?

Ceme-trees.

What type of music do mummies like best?

Ragtime.

What type of music do zombies like best?

Soul music.

What do ghosts use to type letters?

A type-frighter.

What was the skeleton rock band called?

The Strolling Bones.

What was the wizard's favourite band?

ABBA-cadabra.

185

What's a vampire's favourite dance?

The fangdango.

What don't zombies wear
on boat trips?

Life jackets.

What's three metres tall, has twelve fingers, three eyes and wears sunglasses?

A monster on summer vacation.

What's a skeleton's favourite musical instrument?

A trom-bone.

Where do Australian ghosts live?

In the Northern Terror-tory.

Where do ghosts go swimming?
In the Dead Sea.

Which ghost is President of France?
Charles de Ghoul.

Who did the witch call when her
broom was stolen?

The flying squad.

Who finished last at the
Yeti Olympics?

Frosty the Slowman.

Why did Dracula take some medicine?

To stop his coffin.

First witch: 'My, hasn't your little girl grown!'

Second witch: 'Yes, she's certainly gruesome.'

Who is big and hairy, wears a dress and climbs the Empire State Building?

Queen Kong.

Who is King of the Cannibals?

Henry the Ate.

Who is the King of the Wizards?

William the Conjurer.

Who won the race between Count Dracula and Countess Dracula?

It was neck and neck.

Why are Cyclops couples happy together?

Because they always see eye to eye.

Why are ghosts always tired?

Because they are dead on their feet.

Why couldn't the witch race her
horse in the Witches' Derby?

Because it was having a spell.

Why did the demon jump into the
conserve?

Because he was a jammy devil.

Why do witches fly on broomsticks?
Because it's better than walking.

Why did the witches go on strike?
Because they wanted sweeping reforms.

Why did the executioner go to
work early?

To get a head start.

Why did the vampire go to
the orthodontist?

To improve his bite.

Why did the young vampire follow
his dad's profession?

Because it was in his blood.

Why didn't the skeleton want to go
to work?

Because his heart wasn't in it.

Why didn't the skeleton bother
to defend itself in court?

Because it didn't have a leg to stand on.

Why do ghosts like the Spice Girls?

Because they're an all-ghoul band.

Why can ghosts speak Latin?

Because it's a dead language.

Why did the zombie decide
to stay in his coffin?

He felt rotten.

Why do skeletons drink milk?

Because it's good for the bones.

Why do witches get good bargains?

Because they're good at haggling.

Why don't ghosts bother telling lies?

Because you can see right through them.

Why is Count Dracula skinny?

Because he eats necks to nothing.

Why isn't the Abominable Snowman
scared of people?

Because he doesn't believe in them.

What do vampires cross the sea in?

Blood vessels.

What did King Kong say when
his sister had a baby?

Well I'll be a monkey's uncle.

What happened when the
Abominable Snowman ate hot pepper?

He melted.

What's green, sits in the corner
and cries?

The Incredible Sulk.

What do you call a good-looking,
kind and considerate monster?

A complete failure.

What do sea monsters eat for lunch?

Potato ships!

Why did the Cyclops give
up teaching?

Because he only had one pupil.

What do Italian ghosts eat?

Spookgetti.

What do you call a sleeping monster
who won't stay quiet?

Frankensnore.

What happened to Frankenstein's
monster when he was caught
speeding?

*He was fined $50 and dismantled
for six months.*

What's a vampire's favourite dog?

A bloodhound!

What happened to the monster that took the five o'clock train home?

He had to give it back.

What do you get when you cross a vampire and a snowman?

Frostbite!

What do you get when you cross a skunk with Frankenstein?

Stinkenstein!

Which ghost ate the three bears' porridge?

Ghouldilocks.

What did the baby zombie
want for his birthday?

A deady bear.

What did the vampire say when
he had bitten someone?

'It's been nice gnawing you!'

What do you do with a green monster?

Put him in a paper bag till he ripens.

What is Dracula's favourite
ice-cream flavour?

Vein-illa!

Why didn't the skeleton cross the road?

Because he didn't have the guts!

What do you call a lamb
with a machine gun?

Lambo.

What did the alien say to the petrol pump?

Take your finger out of your ear when I'm talking to you.

Why don't turkeys get invited to dinner parties?

Because they use fowl language.

What do you get when you cross
a rooster with a steer?

A cock and bull story.

What animal builds his house in
the jungle?

A boa constructor.

What do you call an elephant
that never washes?

A smellyphant.

What do you get if you cross
a skunk with a bear?

Winnie the Poo.

What swings through the trees
and is very dangerous?

A chimpanzee with a machine gun.

How did the skunk phone his
mother?

On a smellular phone.

What do you call a group of people
that dig for bones?

A skeleton crew.

What did the floor say to the desk?

I can see your drawers.

What's brown and sticky?

A stick.

What's the hardest part
about skydiving?

The ground!

Why didn't the man die when he
drank poison?

Because he was in the living room.

What do you get if you pour
hot water down a rabbit hole?

Hot cross bunnies.

Why did the one-handed
man cross the road?

He wanted to get to the secondhand shop!

What's a lion's favourite food?

Baked beings.

Mum: 'Haven't you finished filling the salt shaker yet?'

Son: 'Not yet. It's really hard to get the salt through all those little holes!'

John: 'Have you noticed your mother smells a bit funny these days?'

Will: 'No. Why?'

John: 'Well, your sister told me she was giving her a bottle of toilet water for her birthday!'

How did the dentist become a brain surgeon?

His drill slipped.

What did the undertaker say to his girlfriend?

'Em-balmy about you!'

What has four wheels and flies?

A garbage truck.

How do you make a Venetian blind?

Poke his eyes out.

Person 1: 'Pssst. Do you want to buy the genuine skull of Julius Caesar?'

Person 2: 'You sold me his skull last week. Besides, that one is smaller.'

Person 1: 'This is when he was a boy.'

Person 1: 'I've never been so insulted in all my life.'

Person 2: 'You haven't been trying.'

That dress fits you like a glove.
It sticks out in five places.

The guy who invented the hokey-pokey died, but they couldn't get him into the coffin. His right leg was in, then his right leg was out, his right leg was . . .

When do you put a frog in your sister's bed?

When you can't find a mouse.

What happens when the
Queen burps?

She issues a royal pardon.

What do you call a man with an
elephant on his head?

Squashed.

What's the nearest thing to silver?

Lone Ranger's bottom.

A man went out for a walk and came across a little boy pulling his cat's tail.

'Hey you!' he shouted.
'Don't pull the cat's tail!'

'I'm not pulling,' replied the boy. 'I'm only holding on – the cat's doing the pulling!'

What goes in pink and comes out blue?

A swimmer on a cold day!

What did the royal taster say after drinking the poisoned water?

Not much!

What do well-behaved young lambs say to their mothers?

'Thank ewe!'